Cornering Sales Success

How To Use The Intersection Of Facts And Relationships To INCREASE Sales And BROADEN Distribution

DARRYL ROSEN

DEDICATION

To the great professionals in the beverage industry who have shared their stories with me. Without you, none of this would be possible!

CONTENTS

INTRODUCTION

Is relationship selling dead?

That's a question I ask managers and sales professionals alike.

The answer, of course, is that relationship selling is far from dead.

And if that's the case, one would assume that if you return phone calls and emails promptly, share relevant product information and stop by with doughnuts every once in a while, you should be good to go sales-wise. Correct?

Well, not exactly!

What about fact-based selling? Is that the ticket? Inundating your customers with loads of graphs, sales information, industry data and Nielsen reports. Throw all that on your customer's desk and wait for the orders to flow. Right? Is that all it takes to be successful?

Again, not exactly!

I'd argue that it takes a combination of facts and relationships. I'd argue that sales will increase and you'll corner sales success by spending as much time as possible at the intersection of facts and relationships.

That's where this book will take you.

Before you get started, I'd like to share a couple of points and say thanks for reading this far (which is further than my wife and 3 boys did).

1) There are 50 lessons on these pages. Each lesson is purposely less than 400 words. On the Internet, where everything is 100% factual, I learned that the average person reads approximately 250 words a minute. That means, if my math is correct, you'll be able to get through each lesson in less than 2 minutes. I did that intentionally. It's not that I don't have more to say, but I know that you're busy. Now there won't be any excuses for not reading. (Well, maybe fewer excuses.)

2) As with my other critically acclaimed (by my family...) books, in this prize- winner, I end each chapter with the phrase "That's just the way it works." Prior to my favorite expression, I'll (try to) make a point that's revolutionary in its simplicity. It will have something to do with your success in sales - something to do with increasing sales and broadening distribution.

Well, I have to go now because I'm nearing 400 words. A promise is a promise. Enjoy these pages, and make sure to stop by www.corneringsalessuccess.com for more tools to help YOU find the intersection of facts and relationships.

Spend your time there and you'll INCREASE sales and BROADEN distribution.

That's just the way it works!

1 ACT LIKE A MOTIVATIONAL SPEAKER

Recently I asked some members of my group if they considered themselves to be motivational speakers.

One guy responded vehemently, "I'm not a motivational speaker!"

He was almost offended. (It was a bit disturbing to me . . .)

At any rate, I'd like to ask you the same question: Are you a motivational speaker?

No?

I disagree. I believe that under your façade is a motivational speaker waiting to get out.

Let's dig a bit deeper on this. When I say "motivational speaker," what image does that conjure up? A packed stadium with a fast-talking, entertaining speaker pacing the stage from side to side inspiring members of the audience to chase their dreams? Is that what you see? Do you see Colin Powell or Da Coach (former Bears coach Mike Ditka) imploring you to do something productive with your life?

As you imagine such a speaker, what traits might this individual display? On the following page is the list I typically get when I ask my groups how they'd describe a motivational speaker.

- Gives direction
- Displays leadership
- Is encouraging
- Is productive
- Leads by example
- Is goal orientated
- Shows fairness
- Is easy to understand
- Is easy to relate to
- Offers constructive comments
- Is punctual
- Has presence
- Displays positivity
- Has confidence
- Is informative
- Is honest
- Gives inspiration
- Displays credibility
- Has a clear message

Then I ask the group again: Are *you* motivational speakers?

More hands go up, but not everyone is convinced.

Here's the truth. Whether you manage two people or two hundred people or none at all, you should consider yourself a motivational speaker.

It's time to start thinking like one.

You have the ability to take people to a better place. I know you're always trying to get someone to do something! And that doesn't require *being* a motivational speaker, but it does require *thinking* like one...

That's just the way it works!

2 ADD VALUE BEFORE ASKING FOR VALUE

Recently I was asked the following two questions about my experiences as a wine, beer and spirit retailer:

1. Did you ever hide from a sales professional?
2. What would make you hide from a sales professional?

Yes, of course I hid from sales professionals, and I remember exactly where I hid - in the warehouse right behind a pallet of vodka or something similar. The *why* part is a little more complex.

Why would I hide from somebody just trying to do his job? What would cause me to go to such great lengths? What type of sales professional would I hide from?

The sales professionals whom I hid from were the ones who always asked me for something. The ones who always wanted value from me but conveniently forgot to give me any value. The types who failed to read the social cues and never offered to help me in some way out of the goodness of their hearts, as opposed to for the benefit of their wallets. The people who always expected me to reach in my pocket each and every time they stopped by.

You know the type: The people who get the order and quickly move on to the next nameless, faceless notch on the way to their year-end bonus. The self-serving pretenders. Sales professionals who don't add any value to the process and who resemble a vending machine.

Not the valued partners.

Don't get me wrong. I understand that sales professionals have to sell. That is a given – it's how they put food on the table. I'm simply suggesting that sales professionals don't have to sell every time they stop in an account. That builds resentment. That builds the perception that the sales professional is just out for himself and, unfortunately, perception is reality in these types of selling situations.

Sometimes, your customers need a breather.

The worst label a sales professional can earn is that he's only out for the immediate sale.

That's just the way it works!

3 ADMIT YOUR ERRORS

Remember the sitcom *Happy Days*?

For those of you who weren't watching TV in the '70s, *Happy Days* was a '50s-era sitcom featuring Arthur Fonzarelli - the ultra-cool, motorcycle-riding, chick magnet affectionately known as "The Fonz."

"The Fonz" (in his mind) was never wrong. Never. And if he was...he certainly couldn't admit it. "The Fonz" couldn't say he was wrong no matter how hard he tried.

"I was wr..........," he would stammer and stutter. It was pretty funny!

Anyway, here's my question:

How do you handle your errors? Do you admit your mistakes? Blame others? Blaming others feels good in the short term but certainly does you no favors in the long run. Do you tell others how badly you feel? Do you beg for forgiveness?

Errors are not always a death sentence. In fact, if you resolve errors the right way, you can actually build stronger relationships with your team, your boss, and your customers.

"Own up" as quickly as possible. Let your team and customers hear about the error from you, not from others. Otherwise, you'll be seen as a procrastinator and a coward. If your idea of acknowledgment is *passing the buck*, then you'll be seen as a bigger coward, and your colleagues will assume that the mistake is greater than it actually is. By the way, when you admit weakness, you'll be portrayed more humanly, and others will be more sympathetic. After all, they have weaknesses, as well.

Just a quick look at our nation's history shows that some very important people, including presidents, have admitted weaknesses and still survived, sometimes even with an enhanced reputation. Contrary to some thinking, admitting your mistakes is a sound practice to strengthen your leadership presence.

So get it off your chest and fix it. You'll look THAT much better in your customer's eyes.

That's just the way it works!

4 ASK FOR THE SALE - AGAIN

Max had been selling for 3 short months when he asked me the following question:

"When presenting a new product, if the customer says "no," is it ok to re-present the same product at a later date?"

I understand his trepidation. He doesn't want to turn off his customer by being too pushy.

To Max, I say, **"Of course it's ok to re-present the product!** If you weren't successful on your first attempt, so what? It took Thomas Edison over 100 tries to get a light bulb to work. Nobody achieves all his or her goals on the first try. Often, it takes many attempts."

However, after the sales call (as soon as possible), Max should try to determine what he could have done differently.

In other words, what could have gone better? Was there something in his approach? Was he prepared? Was he on time for the meeting? Did he have an (interesting) interest-gaining statement of some substance? Did the buyer seem rushed or harried?

This is a time for soul-searching. Some sales professionals will blame everybody else (including, sadly, their mothers) for their inability to close the deal. It's always somebody else's fault. Don't fall prey to that unproductive thinking. Take responsibility. Assume, in a positive way, that you merely have to do things differently next time to make the sale.

After a short period of time, *feel free to re-present the product*, *but not until you have come up with a creative way to get your customer juiced.*

Let's say that once more for EMPHASIS. **It's ok to re-present**. Go ahead; but don't do so until you've re-engineered your approach.

Remember: unless your product is the second coming of (insert any fantastically exceptional product introduced during the last 10 years), your customers probably would rather encounter the bubonic plague than sign a purchase order. How many selections can they have on the drinks menu? How high can their shelves go?

Put yourself in their shoes. Step outside of the "my product is perfect" mentality! What would excite you? What would get you to pull the trigger?

So, there you have it, Maxwell! It's not over until it's over and I don't hear anyone singing! Keep asking for the sale. If you execute in a thoughtful and creative manner, your customer will appreciate your persistence.

I know I always did.

That's just the way it works!

5 BE "OF VALUE" TO YOUR CUSTOMERS

Close your eyes and imagine the following:

It's a clear, high-definition image of your most important customer.

Wow, what a clear picture! He's seeing sales professionals like you all day long. It's like the Indy 500 in there; he's got them booked back-to-back-to-back. And you thought your day was busy. Man, this guy is getting it from all directions - customers, vendors, his boss, his employees, people in corporate. Of all the humanity!

He can't possibly be giving them all his undivided attention. Can he? Is that possible?

Absolutely not! Not even close, and the key questions are: to whom is he giving the greatest share of his attention? To whom is he giving half his attention?

And most important: **who is on the pay-no-mind list?**

Here's the take-away: there IS a pay-no-mind list and I **don't** want your name on that list. While all the lessons in this book are about how to add value and be "of value," it's imperative that you know early on, like in lesson 5, that such a "list" exists.

Now back to our regularly scheduled guidance.

You know that your customers don't listen to all their vendors with the same degree of attention. They listen to some more than others. They listen to the sales professionals they perceive to be "of value" to them.

So while you might think you're knocking it out of the park on a sales call, your customer may not even be listening. Oh, it may seem that he's listening, but it's likely that you don't have his undivided attention. Your job (your goal) is to be the one he listens to – out of all the vendors rearing their ugly heads that day. (Not your ugly head, mind you, their ugly heads.)

You may think you're different, you may think that you're better than the competition, you may think you're "of value"...

However, if your customer can't identify what you stand for or how you're better than the competition or what you're good at...

...you may be just like everyone else. And that's a terrible place to be.

That's just the way it works!

6 BE ENTHUSIASTIC

Is there such a thing as being too gung-ho about your products?

A few years back, our family purchased a new car. My son Josh went with me to pick up the car, and while we waited, one of the dealership's veterans (Henry) went over the car's features with us.

Henry waxed poetic about the car. It seemed like he was deriving an inordinate amount of pleasure describing the car, even when showing us how to open the trunk. Clearly, he wanted to make sure we were comfortable with the new car, but his behavior went beyond that.

This got me thinking: Is there such a thing as being too gung-ho about your products? Henry probably really likes Honda automobiles. Maybe he even likes his job. But what really got my attention about his extreme enthusiasm (and prevented it from being too unnerving) was that it seemed genuine.

What about you? Can your customers tell how you think and feel about your products? If your enthusiasm is manufactured, then your customers will know.

Do you have to love your products? Not necessarily. Do you have to like your products? Not really. Do you have to possess a real belief that your products will make your customers money? *Absolutely* – and you must convey this to your customers.

Enthusiasm must be infectious. You can believe with every breath that your brands are the real deal, but if you're not able to transfer this feeling to your customers, your belief isn't worth a hill of beans — whatever that's worth. I'm not staying current on the price of beans, nor hills for that matter.

But, really, as I scan my past, I can remember so many occasions where a sales professional would sit in front of me, and I could sense that he couldn't care less about his products. In such situations, I was hardly ever moved to purchase.

I figured — if he doesn't care, why should I?

I didn't buy that day and, given similar circumstances, neither will your customers — today or any other day.

That's just the way it works!

7 BE FLEXIBLE

On a sales call, priorities can change in a second, like they might have for many runners just prior to the 2007 Chicago marathon, which took place on a really hot day. Temperatures were hitting 70 degrees at the start of the race and approaching 85 degrees with suffocating humidity by mid-day. I have never run a marathon under such extreme conditions, although I once came close. I ran one in 1979 (as a naive 13-year-old) when the mercury topped off at 84 degrees, and I remember the challenges those conditions presented.

The night before that Chicago race, many marathoners were probably eating their pasta and worrying plenty about the race conditions. They were likely making decisions on how to run the following morning. What would you do in that situation? Would you back off your original racing plans or run as fast as you expected to run before the weather was announced. Would you observe the conditions and adjust your plans accordingly? I know what I would do, and, suffice to say, it's probably good that I wasn't running that day!

Those runners with flexible personalities probably changed their plans and aimed simply to survive the elements. The inflexible runners, those who stayed with plans they made prior to learning about the extreme conditions, likely had a pretty tough day! So what do you do when things change before, during, or after a sales call?

Do you change course or dig your heels in?

I understand the "I have to make the sale today" feeling, but sometimes today is not the day. Sometimes you have to stop, adjust course, and gather more information when the customer says "no."

The reality is that you don't always have to make the sale today, and unless you're extraordinarily diplomatic, arguing with your customer can come off as - I don't know - arguing with your customer...

...And arguing rarely leads to a sale!

Instead, come up with a more creative way to re-introduce your products.

Yes, forget the sale today for a sale tomorrow. Set yourself up to re-present and there's a better chance your customer will decide to see it your way...

That's just the way it works!

8 BE MORE SELECTIVE WITH YOUR FAVORS

When I coach young sales professionals, I always ask the following question:

"Are you any better at selling than you were a year ago?"

Ready for the big shock? Most answer **yes,** but the true measure of improvement is their answer to my follow-up question.

How are you better? (This question usually gets 'em!)

Recently, I heard an interesting answer.

The young man I was coaching indicated that he was better at deciphering the end result of doing a favor for a customer. In other words, he got better at being able to sniff out the takers - those who take but don't give.

See, if you've spent any time in the trenches, you know that customers often ask sales professionals to *do them a favor.*

Happens all the time as a matter of fact!

Like anything else, some customers abuse this privilege. They ask and they ask and they ask, but when the sales professional needs something, they suddenly have selective recall.

I was intrigued, talking to this talented, aggressive young professional. He indicated that he had grown tired of this game, so he started working more closely with his customers who understand the concept of quid pro quo.

Now, he grants favors to some but with others, he trades. In other words, he asks for something in return. He doesn't let them get away with an IOU. Does this sound untoward to you? Should sales professionals just do what their customers want in the name of good service?

Perhaps, but resources (and time) these days are scarce, and the best sales professionals learn how to read their customer's intentions. They learn, sometimes the hard way, where to draw the line.

The lesson: save your favors for those who do some *giving* as well as *taking*.

This is a much more equitable way to do business.

That's just the way it works!

9 BUILD RAPPORT THE OLD FASHIONED WAY

Do you use any old-fashioned methods to build rapport with your customers?

Let me explain by telling you about a friend I met long ago.

Everybody who knows me understands that I am a die-hard, long-suffering, Cubs baseball fan. In my old office (in Chicago) were numerous pictures taken at Cubs games.

Everybody who visited my office knew about my fondness for the Cubbies. This included Frank, a sales professional whose business never went very far with us. He never made any real effort to connect. Then, one day, while witnessing another Cubs loss at Wrigley Field, I saw Frank.

After seeing how he was dressed, my jaw just about hit the floor.

Frank was dressed in Cubbie blue from head to toe. He wore blue baseball shoes. He had on pinstripe baseball pants, a blue belt, a mock turtleneck with a Cubs emblem, a regulation jersey and a Cubs hat. (Frankly, it was kind of creepy.) It should come as no surprise that there wasn't a significant other with him.

Anyway, what's important to consider is what happened after that day at Wrigley. Frank and I became friends and went to numerous games together. And his sales with us increased. And when he took me to an away playoff game in Florida (separate rooms, thank you very much), his sales increased yet again.

(Very important note: Frank was strongly dissuaded by the threat of losing ALL my business…from ever wearing a full baseball uniform while sitting near, or in the general vicinity of ME at a game or anywhere else!)

I thought you should know that!

I also want you to understand – this is not a story about buying a customer's business, although I did enjoy the playoff game. It's really about putting yourself in a better position to seize the day with your customers.

During games, Frank and I were building rapport the old-fashioned way. We didn't trade emails, send texts, write on each other's Facebook walls, tweet each other or use Skype. No, we sat face-to-face and shared information the old-fashioned way. I saw the conviction in his eyes when he spoke about his products and how genuinely he felt that his portfolio would help my business.

So, as you navigate through the new channels of communication, make sure that you don't forget what some would call the prehistoric method of communication. You simply can't get to know someone in 140 characters or less.

That's just the way it works!

10 CUT THROUGH THE CLUTTER

Do you ever watch those incredible music award shows?

I remember watching the Black Eyed Peas perform one of their hit songs one year. What an amazing performance, but I found the combination of lights, action and dancing a bit over-stimulating.

It was hard to concentrate on their great music...

...Which reminds me of life today.

I think we all suffer from *collective ADD*.

Think about it, your customers are constantly bombarded with information, and while you may feel that you're breaking through the clutter, that's often not the case.

I suggest the following:

Use the word "YOU" more than "I"
Nothing is more important to the customer than the customer himself. Asking, "What are YOU trying to achieve?" is much better than saying, "This is what I'm trying to achieve."

Use short sentences and short paragraphs
You have such a small window of opportunity to get your point across, so use your words economically. Clarity improves with fewer words. (Provided you consider the next point.)

Use only necessary words

Don't overload the reader with extra adjectives and adverbs. Say only what needs to be said. This is really hard to do, actually, and requires superb editing skills. You'll learn quickly, though, that you don't need to say a ton to get your point across.

Use powerful words

There are certain words that evoke positive reactions. Without turning into a snake oil salesman, it would be wise to spice up your business communication with a few of the following words.

- Absolutely
- Accomplish
- Critical
- Instantly
- Proven
- Simple
- Strong
- Surefire
- Understand
- Unparalleled

When writing emails, writers often forget that readers are busy and that they have little time to go through reams of material. When faced with something daunting, readers will put it aside, conceivably never to look at it again…

…And that's certainly not how you want your communication to be received!

Keep it short, sweet, and to the point and you'll keep their attention.

That's just the way it works!

11 DEVELOP A PERSONAL BRAND

Long ago in a distant land . . . actually, it was just a few miles from here, there lived a man who built a fabulous personal brand.

His brand was information, and he shared much more than anyone else. Plus, this was before the Internet and email, so his materials were more time consuming to produce and deliver. All the printing and photocopying was painstaking, yet every week several people at our company received via snail mail a packet of tasting notes, product specs and Wine Spectator scores.

His personal brand was supplying relevant and useful information in a timely manner, and it paid off for him handsomely.

What's your personal brand? (You knew that question was coming!)

Consider the following list of questions as you determine how to stand apart from the crowd:

- What do you want people to think about you?
- What type of reputation do you want to have?
- What characteristics describe you? (I am...)
- What characteristics shouldn't describe you? (I am not...)
- What's your perception of how the market perceives you?
- What do people genuinely think of you? (Have you asked them?)
- What are people missing? (What do they misunderstand about you?)

- What should you be doing better at? (What bothers you most about your performance?)
- What are your internal barriers? (Do you have any self-imposed roadblocks?)

One more question: Are you using any marketing tools to differentiate yourself and leverage your presence in the marketplace? Do you use social media to build your brand?

(Note: just because you're a sales professional in a mammoth beverage distributor doesn't mean you shouldn't use social media to build your personal brand. Just highlight your employer in a positive light and follow company guidelines. Also, think twice before posting "partying" pictures on Facebook! Yikes!)

The information junkie I described above used knowledge-sharing as a way to stand apart from others. When I was reviewing his materials, I wasn't thinking about his competition. My attention was on him and when push came to shove, he was the person I called when we needed something new and exciting for our shelves.

And that's the purpose of your personal brand – to get those calls.

That's just the way it works!

12 DON'T ACT LIKE A DEAD BEAT DAD

Do you act like a deadbeat dad?

Ok, give me a little latitude here! I promise I'll make a point.

The definition of a deadbeat dad, according to the urban dictionary, is a father who doesn't provide for a family that he helped create. And this type of individual exists in the beverage business - albeit a bit differently.

When placing products, getting the "yes" is fulfilling, but what comes after is more important.

So the question is: do you stick around to build and maintain what you've *created,* or do you act like a *deadbeat dad* (e.g., by quickly moving on to the next account, product or incentive)?

Simply, great service = great selling. Think about it this way. You want to move from a place where customers simply like you to a place where customers VALUE having a relationship with you.

For the purpose of this lesson, let's consider the role of service in that equation.

Here are some ways to deliver great service:

- Return phone calls and emails promptly.
- Give helpful advice BEFORE your customer gets that advice from a competitor.

- Maintain displays – signs and placards, shelves, coolers and all other marketing. Check for accuracy.
- Bring credibility by knowing how your products stand out and what makes them special.
- Handle pricing errors in a timely manner. (Good luck gaining new distribution when your customer is thinking about a 4-dollar credit memo you missed several weeks ago!)
- Go to bat for your customers when problems arise. Don't kick the problem over to the warehouse and go about your day.
- Help move inventory that isn't moving as quickly as you said it would. Look, any sales professional can *estimate* how long it will take to blow through that endcap; however, it takes a truly service-oriented professional to help make it happen. Your question should always be "Am I doing enough to push through inventory?"

And there's much, much more. Anything having to do with sharing profitable ideas is great service.

The service game is an account by account thing – so take out a piece of paper, name 10 accounts and determine what you can do better in each of them. Start small; Rome wasn't built in a day!

Remember, great service equals great selling.

That's just the way it works!

13 FIGHT FIRE WITH PATIENCE

One evening a manager called me during dinner. Usually there's a "no smart phone at the dinner table" policy in our house, but since the kids use theirs...

Anyway, it was a manager who was very upset. He had given an important presentation, and his analysis was attacked vociferously at every turn.

That can be upsetting and humiliating. When that happens to you, take a deep breath and formulate your response.

Always respond with respect and brevity to attacks on your numbers and ideas.

It might be tempting, especially if you've done your homework, to diffuse attacks with tons of data and logic to disprove the other opinion. But if your mouth goes into overdrive, then the atmosphere of *rapt attention* needed to build strong buy-in for your idea will be hard to maintain. The more words you use, the more you fight, and you'll lose your customer's attention in no time.

Do the opposite. Keep your responses clear and short. Allow less time for minds to wander. If the conversation gets heated, don't react to an obvious bully by being a bigger bully. As you attempt to gain approval for your plan, treat others with clear respect.

Understand that when someone attacks your presentation, there could be a bit of fear mongering going on. A fear monger will try to raise dozens of questions, most of which can't be answered well or with any specificity, because he knows that confusion is a splendid strategy for delaying a decision.

Be appreciative of his concerns. The way to respond to *"What about this, and that, and this, and that?"* is to suggest that no idea is 100% certain to work out of the box, while at the same time giving reasons why your idea has a concrete chance of success.

At the end of the day, the more you embrace the naysayers, the more you'll learn about the obstacles. It's far better to get them talking than not talking at all.

That's just the way it works!

14 FOCUS ON WHAT'S MOST IMPORTANT

Before Memorial Day last year, our family stopped by the local Baskin Robbins for ice cream. The line was out the door with just one lonely high school student serving customers.

Instead of helping her, the owner, a crotchety fellow, was refilling the gummi bears. (Wouldn't want to run out of gummi bears...) All the customers could see him standing just off to the side.

The line grew. And grew. I was in line for 20 minutes, and I never saw the owner serve a single customer.

I don't normally do this, but I spoke up. "Think she needs some help???"

I loved his response. *"Have to fill the candy. Can't sell the candy if there is no candy."*

Wow! Well said, and what spectacular customer service skills (sarcasm intended). But really, who eats gummi bears on ice cream? Maybe the red ones are ok, but the entire cast of outlaw colors should stay away.

Anyway, I didn't conduct a survey, but I imagine the customers probably cared more about getting their ice cream BEFORE the holiday ended than being able to order a chewy object that many feel has no place in ice cream. And Cranky, the owner, wasn't paying attention to what was **most important**. (Side note: This sounds harsh, I realize, but I've been going there for years. He's cranky. I know of what I speak!)

Regardless, this story makes me want to ask you the following question:

Do YOU pay attention to what's most important?

I've heard it said - *"There can be only one most important thing. Many things may be important but only one can be the most important."* So, if disproportionate results come from one activity, then you must give that activity a disproportionate amount of your time. Right?

Sadly, I find that many professionals don't follow this script. *They act on a particular belief even when that belief is not the most important thing to focus on.* Small things, like the scary lack of gummi bears, jumble their thinking and misguide their actions.

Don't gum up your success by worrying about gummi bears.

Instead, spend time concentrating on what's important. You'll be able to have your ice cream and eat it, too.

That's just the way it works!

15 GAIN INTEREST FROM DAY 1

If it's not fresh on day one, when is it fresh?

That's my philosophical take on an experience I had a few months ago.

I was with a group of young sales professionals. The crème de la crème. They had just sat through a supplier presentation about an interesting new product. Afterwards, I spoke to them. Since our topic was sales call preparation, I asked the team how they would get me (as a potential customer) jazzed about carrying this new product.

The results were underwhelming to say the least! What struck me was that just 30 minutes earlier they listened to a dynamic presentation about the product. The info was fresh - like a daisy.

I wanted their idea of generating interest to be more interesting than "I have this new product; here are the price sheets." My goal was to learn what they found unique and then to hear them craft an interest-generating statement that would knock my socks off.

My socks stayed on.

Here's my point: To me, if a launch is to be successful, professionals have to know how to generate interest. Aside from samples and prices sheets, how will the sales pro generate interest in a meaningful way?

In this case, the new brand was produced with the following in mind: The brewer wanted consumers to feel (perceive) that his beer costs significantly more than it does. His goal was for there to be an overwhelming (knock your socks off) value upon the first sip.

Given that, my recommendation would be to say, *"How do you feel when you crack open a craft beer, and it tastes so good you immediately question how much money you paid for it?"*

The customer will probably say something along the lines of, "I like that feeling."

"Great, because I tried something recently that's going to knock your socks off!"

YES, it's a bit bizarre, but it's better than "I have something new to show you!" All that statement does is raise your customer's defenses.

The key is to stop a busy customer in his tracks and to give him something to think about. No matter how silly an interest-gaining statement sounds, if you want to stand out, you'll get much further if you generate interest from day 1.

That's just the way it works!

16 GET FEEDBACK FROM YOUR CUSTOMERS

You're so vain; you probably think this song is about you – don't you, don't you?

Remember the catchy tune about vanity by the legendary Carly Simon – a famous singer from a few years back?

Despite the fact that I'm usually advising professionals to turn their perspective outward, this time I'm going to suggest a little vanity.

I suggest that you ask your customers 2 questions.

First, ask your customers *what you're doing well.*

The reason for this question is to make sure you're concentrating on those tasks that are meaningful to your customers. Just because you think something is important doesn't mean that your customers agree. As noted by author Brian Tracy, "The biggest crime is to do something *well* that need not be done at all!"

Well said!

Every day I hear of situations where well-intentioned professionals excel at tasks that aren't important (or wanted) by their customers. The result is time wasted – which is a delicious recipe for disaster. Do you have a lot of disposable time? (I didn't think so!)

Second, ask your customers *what you could do better.*

Look for trends. Are many customers saying the same things? If so, you know where you can improve. If it walks like a duck…you know how that one ends.

Here are a few words of caution as you do this:

- Many customers may automatically (as if conditioned by Pavlov) respond by speaking about price, discounts, or other monetary variables. Push on this. Beyond the world of price, there are always other variables that help your customers make decisions.

- Don't ask the questions if you'll automatically dismiss the answers. That will do more harm than good. "Denial" isn't just a river in Egypt, as they say. Besides, if many customers point out the same issues – take the lesson and run with it.

Accept your customer's comments with a smile on your face. As long as their feedback is well-intended and not vindictive, you can always learn from it.

That's just the way it works!

17 GO FROM "I" AND "ME" TO "YOU"

Does your selling language speak directly to your customers, or is it more about you?

Back in the early 1970s, Yale University commissioned a study to identify the most persuasive words in the English language for the purpose of helping businesses with their marketing. It should come as no surprise that the number one word was **"you."**

It seems like reputable research, so let's start incorporating the word **"you"** into your presentations, in limited doses at first. The benefit to YOU of doing this is that it will force YOU to frame the benefits of carrying your products in your customer's terms. Why they will benefit by carrying the products you suggest. Why it will help their businesses! Why it will attract consumers and create excitement.

But you have to be careful. Make sure YOU'RE using it the right way. Check out the following examples:

Good use: *"You will see that consumers are responding quite favorably to our advertising and will flock in droves to your business to buy this product.* (I know – it's a little hokey but at least your framing the benefit with your customer in mind.)

Bad use: *"You have a terrible craft beer selection, and your business will surely fail if you don't buy our incredible product."*

As you can see, one statement is positive, and the other is purposely quite negative (and mean) and incredibly self-serving.

The point: **Be careful!**   Using phrases like "you always" or "you should" is too personal, too accusatory, and quite condescending.   It's "preachy" and even if you think a particular buying decision is best for a customer, don't frame it that way.   A basic premise in selling is that your customers want to buy your product because *they* think it's a good idea, not because you told them to!

One last point: as you evaluate your statements, try to answer the infamous question **"What's in it for my customer?"**   For example, saying, "I've been doing this for 30 years" means nothing to the customer.

Except that you've grown, shall we say, *mature* doing what you're currently doing!

Instead, say, "I've been doing this for 30 years, and I've seen how the marketplace reacts to products like this one.   This product will do well because…"

You're stating a benefit that comes from your 30 years of experience, which will help your customer make better buying decisions.

And that's taking care of #1. (Not you, silly – your customer!)

That's just the way it works!

18 HAVE A PLAN

Many years ago, I tried to qualify for the Boston Marathon. As you know, they don't let just anyone run the Boston, and to gain entry, you have to run a pretty competitive time.

I thought it would be easy because I ran track and cross country in high school. Can you picture me with hair? Blowing in the wind? Coeds sighing as I run by? Never mind!

To make a long story somewhat bearable, in trying to qualify for Boston, I ran the Chicago Marathon that year and started out way too fast. I know the psychology of marathon running suggests you should pace yourself, but evidently I didn't get that memo.

By 10 miles I was struggling mightily, by 12 miles I was walking, and by 14 miles, I was looking for a taxi. A DNF! (Do you know what that stands for? Let me give you a hint: It's not *Do Not Follow*.)

If one had followed me that day, they wouldn't have gone near the finish line. That much was for sure.

Anyway, that day taught me a huge lesson.

You can't have a goal without a plan or some concrete thought on how to achieve the goal you've set. For me, the goal was qualifying for Boston, but, when push came to shove, I really had no plan for how I was going to get it done.

Do you have a plan?

Each month you get a monster set of goals that seems to grow by the day. How concrete is your plan for achieving your numbers?

Consider this bit of research I picked up some years ago with a few of my comments.

- **70%** of individuals wish to achieve their goals – but that wish is fleeting like the wind.
- **10%** have a strong desire to achieve goals – but that's really the end of their commitment.
- **8%** have high hopes – and dare to imagine from time to time that they might actually get what they want.
- **6%** have a strong belief that they have what it takes.
- **4%** crystallize their wishes, desires and hopes into a burning desire to succeed. (We're getting closer!)

And...

- **2% actually have a plan. (This is where you want to be!)**

So let's put this lesson into practice. When the monthly goals come out, do you prepare a plan for reaching the numbers or do you *wish upon a shining star?*

Making numbers can be intimidating. Not as much, though, if you have a plan.

That's just the way it works!

19 HONE YOUR QUESTIONING TECHNIQUE

Do your questioning skills need work? If so this lesson is for you!

Proper questioning is more than just asking the right questions. It's also about *how* the questions are asked.

Much of the technique starts after your initial query. After asking your initial question, drill down (to learn more) and resist the urge to jump from subject to subject.

Consider how a typical conversation goes: "How's the family?" "Not bad." "How's business?" "Not bad." "Are sales strong?" "Sort of." By employing this style, the questioner is jumping from topic to topic and getting nowhere on even one particular subject.

Think about the following: Imagine that you ask, "How is the promotion working out?" Your customer may answer, "Good." A questioner who jumps around would then ask a completely unrelated question like, "What's going on with that new line of wines?"

Instead, follow up by saying, "Why is it good?" or "Good – how?" As you ask and listen, your goal is to reflect on the reasons why the promotion is working so you can apply that knowledge to other situations. You can't glean that information if you gloss over the answers by quickly moving on to another topic.

It's best not to assume too much and fill in the blanks for your customers. If Jean says, "Business is soft," don't immediately offer up YOUR perception as to why she's seeing that softness. Ask a few questions to get her perspective. Ask, "Why is it soft?" or "What part of your business is soft?" Use her words for maximum impact. If Jean says, "Things are terrible!" ask "Terrible in what way?"

It may seem awkward to use the word "terrible" in that manner; however, repeating the word your customer used shows that you're listening.

Another aspect of honing your questioning technique is asking open-ended questions in a very specific way to get your customer to share more with you.

Here are five suggestions for how to begin open-ended questions:

- **What makes you choose...**
- **What do you like about...**
- **What have you found...**
- **What do you look for...**
- **How are you currently...**

Certainly, there are other variations, but this is a good start. You can literally begin hundreds of different questions with these five suggestions.

Make sure to let the silence do the heavy lifting. If you ask and answer your own question, you'll defeat the entire purpose. Instead, be patient, and your improved questioning technique will pay dividends.

That's just the way it works!

20 IDENTIFY AND SOLVE PROBLEMS

Do you offer solutions BEFORE you learn your customer's problems?

Over time, as sales professionals and managers, most of us have been trained to state the benefits of the products we sell. Some where along the way, it was beaten into our heads, and now it's the method most people default to when they go to market.

So we're effectively leading with a solution that may or may not fit the problem we think we know about.

It's confusing, I know.

We should be leading with the problem.

Here's how it works:

Our brains are always on the lookout for possible problems, going back even to the prehistoric days of hunting and gathering. We're naturally attracted to problems first, and it's only when we see the obvious—and possibly the most appropriate—solution that we start to relax.

Identifying the problem comes first.

But what if there's no obvious problem? (Should you drum one up?)

Well, no.

It's not the best strategy to scare customers into buying your products.

But you do need to highlight any real problems that exist, so you can show how your product fits the bill. In the meantime, you're also showing your customers how their (business) lives can be better, if they adopt your products.

Don't forget – not only is the customer looking for a solution (to a problem) but he also wants to know that the sales professional understands the intricacies of his business.

(That would be you. Do you know the intricacies of his business?)

Because if you do, you'll become "of value" to your customers.

And being "of value" is key, because your customers have dozens of problems running rampant in their brains and dozens of people throwing solutions at them – every day.

To stand out – it's best to isolate the problem and focus on the right solution for that one problem.

That's just the way it works!

21 LEARN SOMETHING ON EACH CALL

Picture the following scenario: Imagine you and a colleague are walking out to the car after an important call. You turn to your colleague and ask, "Did we learn anything of substance about our customer?"

What would the answer be?

If you asked some insightful questions and listened intently to the answers, then you probably learned something. You may be of more "value" to your customer.

If you've expanded the professional relationship, then you've used the time effectively. If you've gained pertinent information about the customer, including his goals, passions, and struggles, then good for you. If you've gained a sense of where your business together is heading, nicely done.

If you asked a question he's never been asked before – awesome!

If you insulted your customer…Not so good!

I remember some guy I'd never met with before telling me, "Darryl, you were up 10%, but the market was up 15%. You're underperforming!"

Nicely done, Pal! **(I'll show you underperforming!)**

Other questions to consider:

- Was your presentation customized or canned?
- Did you educate?
- Have you **connected the dots** to learn what really makes this business tick?
- Did you hit the specifics? Do you understand your customer's investment? Inventory turns? Did you talk intelligently about the numbers?
- Did you learn how **his** performance is measured - customer count, profit, ROI, etc. - and how you can help? Are you in a better position to add value?

For better or worse, you don't get as many uninterrupted customer touches as you'd like in a year, so it's best to walk away from a call learning more about your customer than who he thinks is going to win the Super Bowl. (Though everyone already...Da BEARS!)

That's just the way it works!

22 LISTEN

The afternoon duo on the sports radio station here in Chicago is very entertaining. Sometimes a caller will phone in and allege that the hosts said something outrageous. The hosts, having said nothing of the sort, will ask if the caller has been listening to an "imaginary radio." If the caller stubbornly continues, the hosts may quickly hang up, but only after shouting, *"Listening is a skill!"*

(I wish the imaginary radio would play a Cubs World Series game, but since that's not going to happen, let's get back to reality.)

Good listening skills are a valuable tool, one that will help you connect with your customers. These skills will help you become a priority and more "of value" to them.

How are your listening skills?

Do you actively listen during conversations, or does your mind wander? Are you thinking of what to say when your turn rolls around? Are you constantly interrupting others?

Yes, listening is a skill, and we can build yours by considering the following:

- **Maintain eye contact**

Try not to let your gaze wander. Your conversation partner needs to know that you're paying attention. Don't stare, though. That's creepy.

- **Incorporate gestures**

Nod your head when appropriate. Do this naturally, not like a puppet with someone else at the controls. Use your hands. Incorporating proper gestures will show that you're listening.

- **Remove distractions**

Put your iPhone in your pocket or purse and leave it there. Nothing is so urgent that you must answer your phone every time it rings, even if your spouse is calling to see what you want for dinner. Especially when your spouse is calling to see what you want for dinner.

- **Don't interrupt**

Nothing is more irritating for both customers and colleagues than having someone else finish *their* sentences. Let people vent. Let them complete their sentences. Hold your tongue even if you know what they're going to say because they've said it hundreds of times before.

- **Concentrate**

Focus on what your customers are saying, *not* what you're going to say. This isn't a throwaway point. You can nod appropriately and hold your tongue, but if you're not concentrating, you're not hearing what is said and what is left unsaid.

Simply, the easiest way to persuade your customers to listen to you more is to listen to them more.

That's just the way it works!

23 LIVE IN THE PRESENT

A few years ago I was asked to help Lucy improve her success rate for placing new items.

I remember her manager telling me that Lucy would invent every reason under the sun about why her customers wouldn't buy her new products: This customer won't like it because of the package. This customer doesn't buy white wines. This customer prefers the other distributor.

She was letting *yesterday* dictate **unsupported** conclusions about why her customers wouldn't bite *today*. What she really needed to do instead was to create a compelling case and ask for the order.

Do you prejudge customers?

Deciding not to show customers certain products equates to prejudging them and essentially saying "No" on their behalf.

(One quick sidebar at this point: Obviously, if your customer doesn't like a certain category of product, don't bring selections from that category week after week. That's offensive. However, my message here is that if you let the past rule the present, over time you'll have nothing left to sell.)

At any rate – let's go back to our prejudging sales professional. When she shifted her focus to *today*, she overcame emotional hurdles and put to use a wider range of sales tools: she got to know more people in her accounts, and she made a greater effort to know the customer's likes and dislikes. She looked for voids in her customer's selection and asked questions that forced her customers to think. She learned more about her own products, and her pre-call preparation soared to a whole new level. As a result, she learned more about her customer's goals, passions, and challenges.

She learned to "live in the moment," and your professionals can do the same. Though their natural inclination might be to talk themselves out of the sale every day of the week, a focus on *today* will lead to a better approach. Live in the moment and ask for the order. That's how you place new items!

That's just the way it works!

24 LOOK FOR OPPORTUNITY (DRIVE)

Very early one morning, I was driving through Minnesota. With my one open eye I read the following sign along the highway:

Opportunity Drive – 10 miles

I thought, "That's it! The answer to the whole 'where do I find more opportunity' question is just a few miles away. Sure am glad I took this highway."

I wish it were that easy.

You know that your ability to harvest opportunities is the lifeblood of your sales existence. Right?

So, without further ado, here are a few things to keep in mind.

- Ask – where is the opportunity at this company?

- Let the account history be your floor, not your ceiling. Be spontaneous and alert. Take the blinders off.

- Study the competition. What are they doing differently? What are they doing well that you should be doing?

- Create missionaries and converts. Plan more events and staff education. Find individuals who believe in your products and are willing to preach the gospel (so to speak.)

- Pop the question. Don't say "no" for your customer. Let them decide. .

- Avoid *friendly fire* - the envy, jealousy, infighting and jockeying that occurs in most companies, for whatever reason. Instead, roundtable with your teammates and ask what is working well in their world?

- Be more aware of the tools your company has to sell its products.

- Spend less time at the drive-through window. Do a better survey. Strive for more face time. Walk the account. Take your time.

Spend more time thinking. If nothing else, sit in a coffee shop one morning with a blank piece of paper. Write down the name of an account, and don't get up until you've emptied your mind of ideas – or until your coffee gets cold.

Using these approaches, you'll find that *opportunity Drive* isn't 10 miles away; it's just around the corner.

That's just the way it works!

25 MAKE A DIFFERENCE

Can one person make a difference?

When my son Danny entered high school, he wanted to join a glamour sport . . . so he joined the cross country team. (Football? Really?)

Anyway, being a lifelong runner myself (and a former high school runner of considerably average ability), to say that Danny's involvement in cross country is exciting for me is an understatement. As I listened to the coach during the first parents' meeting, I came to a few stark realizations.

Danny is going to crush my times...

That was only the first revelation. The bigger one was this: The team's performance is important to the coach (and I'm sure he fancies a trip Downstate this fall), but that's not the limit to how he sees his role. He sees it as much more. Building character. Helping young men make good choices and develop healthy habits. Creating future leaders. Encouraging these boys to realize their potential.

And that's the beauty of leadership. We all have the ability to interpret our roles.

All jobs have specific responsibilities. A housekeeper in a fancy Manhattan hotel can see her role as changing sheets and cleaning toilets but, if she wants to, she can see her role as much more than that. She can view her role as doing her part to ensure that her guests have everything they need for a wonderful stay, rather than seeing it narrowly as one who cleans up after others. It's her choice! That's a decision she gets to make herself.

Danny's coach takes a similarly broad perspective. He sees himself as a molder of young men.

Does he actually "reach" his runners with his higher-level goals?   I believe so. Recently he received a note from a former runner who is now in the military. The letter concluded with these words: *"I need to step out of my comfort zone and not take the easy road out. You taught me that, Coach!"*

Yes, one person can make a difference! It just depends on how you see your role.

That's just the way it works!

26 MAKE EVERY MESSAGE COUNT

I see many supplier presentations each year.

Quite frankly, many of these presentations are terrible. I say this not to condemn any professional who hasn't received training in presentation skills, but because it's sad to me.

It's sad because this professional will probably have just one crack at the sales team. One crack at getting the group juiced about her products. One opportunity to make her products stand out among ALL the other products.

One chance to inspire.

But it's often wasted.

Here's what I want you to remember: Every time you speak, you have the chance to inspire – please don't waste it.

Any time you stand in front of a group of people (whether selling or presenting), you're held to a higher standard. Your goal is for your ideas to be accepted and acted upon – not rejected.

Your audience wants that, as well. They want **you** to lead them to a better place.

Your facts don't speak for you. Your PowerPoint slides don't, either.

You speak for you.

Vision, direction and passion – that's what you're after.

So ask yourself the following:

- What image am I projecting?
- Am I energizing my audience?
- Am I interesting?
- How are my presenting skills? (Am I speaking to someone directly? Good presenters make a point directly to someone in the group, not to the carpet or the walls or the ceiling!)
- Am I saying anything controversial? (Run-of-the-mill is safe; however, it's much more engaging to say something controversial and defend the point for all you're worth.)
- Does my audience know that I care? (Beyond being knowledgeable about a subject, do I show that I understand their challenges?)
- Am I solving a problem for my audience? Am I helping them achieve a goal?
- Is there a "big idea"?
- *And most important: Am I leaving my group better off than before?*

Even if you're just there to sell something, you still have the opportunity through your words, actions and delivery to make a difference.

So seize that opportunity. Answer the questions I've posed, and let people know why your thoughts and ideas are good for them.

Once they know WIIFM (What's In It For Me), they'll be ready to take your lead.

And that's the whole point!

That's just the way it works!

27 MAKE LEMONADE FROM LIFE'S LEMONS

Many years ago, my family and I took our first-ever trip during the Christmas season. Since I was in retail and working long hours during December, we were almost never able to get away at that time. We usually stayed in Chicago, but this year we were going to be relaxing by a pool in the hot Florida sun. (SPF 1000, of course, I mean, look at me!)

During the plane ride down, I read a great book on positive thinking. Little did I know how quickly it would come in handy!

We weren't accustomed to the throng of warm-weather seekers, as we had never traveled in December before. The line at the car rental counter seemed longer than the Mississippi River. We waited patiently (mostly) for 45 minutes, only to learn that we were at the wrong place!

Have you ever made a bone-headed move like that? Have you done something that left you scratching your head or pulling out your hair (if you have any left, unlike me)? Typically, these events would have thrown me for a complete loop; however, I was able to draw upon what I had read just a few hours earlier!

"Good news and bad news," I told my family. "The bad news: we're at the wrong car rental place! The good news is that when you want to make fun of me, you now have more material!"

The children weren't impressed. Neither was the wife, as it turns out.

Instead of taking the bus back to the airport, I ended up running a mile to where I should have gone in the first place. At least I got a workout in!

Here's the point: Situations in life can either be positive or negative, happy or sad. You have all heard the expression, "When life gives you lemons, make lemonade." I believe that. Do you? It's your frame of reference that makes the difference. Had I ended up being upset by this fiasco, it would have been my choice!

That's just the way it works!

28 MAKE USE OF DASHBOARD TIME

I imagine you log a lot of time in the car. During these times, what do you do? Do you listen to Howard Stern? Call the spouse? Sing the words to a heartwarming duet? You know, like "Endless Love" or "Next Time You Fall in Love"?

Hey, no wise cracks! Everyone needs a guilty pleasure like lavender bath salts or pickles . . . or duets!

Anyway...

Long stretches in the car are great opportunities to reflect on how you're approaching your vocation. So next time, turn down the radio and contemplate the following questions:

- **Do I see things from my customer's point of view?**

Do I ever *walk in their shoes*? Do my customers genuinely know that I care about them, their businesses, and their associates, or do my actions indicate I only care about myself? What was the last tangible suggestion I gave to help my customers improve their businesses?

- **How well do I know my products?**

Is there something I know about my products that might intrigue my customers? What is it? Am I able to answer customers' questions about my products on the spot?

- **If I made calls for an extra half hour today, what would happen?**

If I planned my day out the night before, what would happen? Would I be better organized? Would I sell more?

- **How well do I listen to my customers?**

Really listen, so I can hear them and understand them? What would happen if I more often let them finish their sentences? Am I constantly jumping to conclusions? Am I a serial-interrupter?

- **What can I do differently?**

Is there something my competitor does (within reason, and the law) that I should be doing? Do I know about the other sales professionals in my accounts? Their strengths; their weaknesses?

You get the picture. It doesn't have to be complicated, and it's not rocket science.

Instead of staring at the dashboard and trying to hit the high notes, THINK! It will be time well spent.

That's just the way it works!

29 MAXIMIZE BUSINESS REVIEWS

I've sat through my share of business reviews. Most left me with only a scant memory of what transpired, but I do remember one with a large spirit supplier like it was yesterday. The "review" consisted of their team and me watching a 45-minute video about the greatness of the company and its founder. By the end of the video, I didn't want to help the company; I wanted to find a way to prevent their success!

Just joking (sort of).

Anyway, I feel that many business reviews are squandered opportunities - the waste of a chance to *talk shop* with a customer, learn critical information and move your "mutual" business forward.

To me, business reviews often felt like glorified infomercials - plastic, boring, and self-serving. And the irony was that the meeting time would have been such a good opportunity to talk business in a setting unencumbered by the usual hodge-podge of issues covered in a traditional sales call.

(e.g. missed deliveries, miscommunications, incorrect invoices.)

Business reviews represent a unique opportunity to talk in an environment not charged by selling pressure. No consternation, no controversy, no conflict. A relatively neutral setting in which to build, cultivate, and maintain customer relationships.

So I hope that you're walking into the account with the right presentation and mindset - one that ensures you're putting yourself in a position to know more about the customer after the review than you did before.

Make the review more than checking a box on a form. It should be much more than "Hey, we did it! Now lets go get lunch! I get shotgun!"

Get rid of the handout with the fake people shaking hands on the cover sheet and the big words "Thank you" on the last page.

Plan for your business reviews with the goal of learning something tangible. With that customer, it could be your most productive hour of the entire year.

That's just the way it works!

30 NAIL THE MOMENT OF TRUTH

Have you ever heard the *"we have no space"* objection?

Hah, I'm sure you've heard that one a few more times than you care to admit! I remember riding with a young sales professional and talking about the upcoming call.

"What objection will you face on this call?" I asked.

"Uh, *space*. 'I have no space!' That's what this guy always says. He's like a broken record!" the sales pro muttered in a disheartened fashion.

So I asked, "Are you prepared to handle that objection should you hear it today?"

"Of course!"

So we headed inside. The young pro sold according to plan and the customer objected according to plan – like he was following a pre-ordained script.

"Where are we going to put that? You know there's no space!"

Then came a response I didn't expect. My sales pro, the one who was so confident minutes before, had nothing to say at this moment of truth. Zilch. Nada. Nothing. He had heard that objection countless times, yet he had no reply. It was as if he had never met this customer before or that it was his very first sales call ever. (I wasn't sure which!)

Anyway, here's my question to you:

Are you prepared to handle the moment of truth? Are you prepared to respond to the most commonly given objections? Are you ready to handle what the customer throws at you?

I'd begin by writing down every single objection your customer might voice. (Great team exercise, by the way.) Use this list of negatives when designing your presentation, and develop positive responses to each objection.

Keep in mind that many people say **"no"** as an automatic defense mechanism. They may not understand . . . they may be confused . . . they may lack confidence . . . many just don't want to seem impulsive!

Instead of throwing in the towel at the moment of truth, keep probing for more information. Even if you've heard that objection five thousand times, hold your tongue. Listen.

And remember: When your customer starts in with a bunch of questions, your responses will be much smoother if there's a plan in place.

That's just the way it works!

31 NAME THE PERCEIVED OBJECTION

I love the Austin Power's movies.

There's a great scene in one of the movies where everyone's hero, Dr. Evil, is waxing on about his bizarre father and even more bizarre upbringing. He talks about how his father claimed outrageous things like "having invented the question mark." I don't think Dr. Evil's father invented the question mark but I could be wrong . . .

Perhaps I should check the Internet!

Anyway, I used to make stuff up also. I used to be able to tell my kids anything and they were none the wiser. They were much younger back then *and* much younger than your customers.

Unfortunately, your customers aren't two years old.

They aren't going to believe everything you say. They will have questions. There will be concerns and even a little confusion. Perhaps also a few misunderstandings, even though I know you're quite thorough and eloquent.

So be proactive. Take the bull by the horns and name the objections up front – before they do. Identify the 800-pound gorilla in the room. Get it out in the open.

Maybe you're thinking – won't that kill the sale?

Au contraire! What *might* kill the sale is acting like what you're selling doesn't raise even a few questions in your customer's mind. What might kill the sale is thrusting out your chest as if to imply that there is nothing wrong with your products or what you're saying.

Underestimating your customers – that's what kills sales. Having no idea of what's important to your customers – that's what kills sales. Hiding from the obvious – that's not going to help much either.

So let's be real here. Your customers are not two-year-olds who accept your every word. As we grow up, we learn quickly that there are two sides to everything, not just coins.

If you bring up the other side before they do, then you'll appear much, much more credible.

That's just the way it works!

32 PERSUADE WITHOUT BEING PUSHY

Here's an interesting question:

"My distributor has been very resistant to making a change that will help our mutual sales. They're more comfortable keeping the status quo, and I find it's almost impossible to teach this old dog a few new tricks. It seems the change I have in mind is something they have no interest in discussing."

Any suggestions?

This is Persuasion 101 at its finest. Unfortunately, many parties in a partnership like yours lack a real ability to force change. Instead, one has to rely on good, old-fashioned persuasion to get something done. Telling a story. Engaging a few hearts. Moving them to a new place. And, as you know, this is quite the challenge because positions get entrenched over time, making change very difficult.

Let's start with one trait (on your part) that won't help you win any battles: Pushiness.

Here's something else that won't work: Being a know-it-all.

Let me explain. Often, what you're suggesting isn't rocket science. In many cases it might be pretty straightforward, and the person you're talking to already knows the best course of action. (Because you've told him or her time and time again!)

But there's something blocking your efforts. Maybe your customer just doesn't see the importance, or perhaps he or she doesn't want to take action for some other reason. Maybe the customer would take action if given a better rationale. Whatever the case, making the change has to be that person's decision, not yours.

Despite your best intentions, your customers don't want your agenda forced upon them. I've repeated this notion several times throughout these lessons because I find that many sales professionals can get pretty *preachy* from time to time. Simply, there is nobody more dangerous than an individual blinded by his or her own point of view.

Come on – you know that brand of assertiveness isn't effective. It won't cause your customer to wake up in the middle of the night and proclaim, "My sales pro is right! I should do what he says."

No, it's going to take a bit more than that!

That's just the way it works!

33 PASS RELATIONSHIP BUILDING 101

Am I doing this right?

It was with an air of exasperation that the young sales professional asked me this question.

He was desperately trying to do all the right things…

It got me thinking.

How do you know if you're building relationships the right way? To be sure, results in an account are a good indication, but absent anything as conclusive as your customer giving you a gold star - it can be kind of confusing.

Here's what to consider. Do you…

- Demonstrate a long-term view of relationships

Many sales professionals prefer seeing results in the short-term. Want to know how your fantasy football team is doing? Look it up! Want the latest Taylor Swift melody? You can have it on your phone in seconds. (Don't judge me. I like her. I love her music…)

Moving on…

…We've been conditioned for quick results but demonstrating a long-term view of relationships will yield better results long term.

- Display a balance between empathy and results

It's difficult being empathetic to your customer's needs while still producing results. However, when you can successfully imagine your customer's needs, you're that much closer to success. When you review your communication, etc. from your customer's perspective, there's a better chance your words/thoughts/ emails will move the ball forward.

- Exhibit a deep knowledge of your customer's business

Not surface stuff but information and insights that will give you the ability to provide valuable insights. Thoughts and ideas that help your customer's business in a tangible way.

- Understand your customer's point of view

How do you react when customers critique your brands? Do you believe that all of your products are perfect? Remember, you're very dangerous when blinded by your own point of view. Your agenda may be laudable, but that doesn't mean you shove it down your customer's throat.

- Employ a genuine caring nature to get closer to your customer.

Some sales professionals get closer to their customers for their own benefit. Other professionals get closer for the customer's benefit or because it's the right thing to do. Only you know the truth; however, when you choose the latter, instead of the former, you've arrived.

That's just the way it works!

34 PRACTICE

Are you ever entrusted with making a critical sales presentation? Perhaps a sales call where your sales manager is in the room or there are some bigwigs from the customer's side? A presentation that involves intricate and detailed programs where you suspect there may be an element of pushback?

I'm always amazed that when faced with a difficult sales call, many talented sales professionals spend more time contemplating which breakfast burrito to eat than considering how to best begin the sales call that has so much riding on it . . . how to start these calls in a manner that gives the sales professional a fighting chance to change or influence a customer's behavior and make the sale.

I often find that this form of pre-call practice is *almost* an afterthought.

So here's the question of the day: **Is it taboo to practice in sales?**

Sometimes I wonder.

What I do know is that professionals in many fields practice. Professional athletes practice. The Chicago Cubs practice! (Well, maybe not so much.) Singers, dancers, wrestlers, comedians, pilots, teachers, public speakers – they all practice. Even I practice. (Maybe more is in order...)

Anyway, the next time you have to say something or sell something - when there's a lot on the line – (Wait for it...)

PRACTICE!

Whatever you plan to say, please, please, please write it down. Practice it some more. And more. Run it by a fellow sales professional or a manager for his or her feedback. Listen to how it sounds.

You probably know from experience that the moment you open your mouth to present, your thoughts are front and center. And the more critical the sale, the more your body will react. Dry mouth, sweaty palms and perspiration in areas where you don't want it; plus, probably some anxiety to boot.

PRACTICE doesn't remove all these uncomfortable reactions, but it does help a great deal. (Deodorant helps, too!)

The most important thing that I want to convey is that what you're saying will always sound better the fifth time you run it through your head compared to the first attempt. Let your customers hear your fifth attempt, not your off-the-cuff remarks. Your results will be much, much better.

That's just the way it works!

35 PREPARE FOR SALES CALLS

No matter where I go, beverage professionals ask me for my "#1 sales secret," as if there exists some kind of magic formula for great sales and flawless execution. Unfortunately, I have no such secrets. I wish I did! However, I do know that better sales call preparation is as close to that secret as I can find.

The formula is simple: **Better Preparation = Better Performance!**

Unfortunately, I've observed many sales professionals who are woefully underprepared for sales calls. They have no idea what their objective is until they open their computer – which often occurs when they're already in front of their customer. When sales professionals use this approach, sales potential is greatly diminished.

Why does this scenario occur? For many reasons (some understandable, some not-so-understandable), sales professionals from all walks of life often think that "winging it" is the way to go.

It's not.

Shooting from the hip doesn't work so well. Having a general idea of what you want to get done is helpful up to a point...

...But the specificity that comes from detailed preparation is far superior!

Many sales professionals rely on the "relationship," which, in this profit- and data-dominated world, loses effectiveness by the day. Even if the retailer is your best friend, he still has to understand the reason that you're

71

selling him a particular item or display.

Hopefully, your rationale isn't "I have a goal" or "I need your help!"

Though your customers may say yes ("just because") to such requests, you still need to educate/inform them so they have more reasons to sell-through the product and to buy and sell more in the future. Profit, sell-through, ROI and other variables are important, and you just don't pull that information out of you-know-where. It takes some advance planning.

If this detailed sales call preparation is not what you're accustomed to doing, start small. Choose one aspect of your preparation routine and go to town on that specific area.

You simply can't juggle all the variables driving sales success while wearing a blindfold. And that's what "winging it" is analogous to - juggling with a blindfold.

That's just the way it works!

36 PRESENT LIKE A PERFORMER

Do you ever have to sell to a large group of people? To some, the prospect of such an activity can remove the living daylights from their bodies. It can be quite intimidating.

Thinking like a speaker or even a performer is often what's needed in order to be memorable and engaging when selling/presenting. With that in mind, here are a few simple strategies for effective presentations, no matter the size of the group.

- **Make sure people are listening**

As a rule, if the people listening to you are crossing their legs, fidgeting, or looking around a lot, chances are you don't have their rapt attention. If you feel that attention is waning, **ask for input**. Solicit opinions. Include everybody.

- **Move around the room**

In college, I used to read the newspaper during large lectures, but when the professor made even the most subtle movement in the direction of my seat, I'd snap to attention and start taking notes again. This can work for you as well. If you establish an unpredictable pattern of movement, people will have no choice but to watch your every move, so I suggest you move around a bit. At the very least, you'll get some exercise.

- **Tell a story**

Paint a picture. In addition to facts and figures, it's helpful to share success stories. One caveat: make sure to ask your customer first to verify that he or she wants that information. They don't always want to hear about another customer's success...

- **Vary your presentation style**

Use different presentation aids to liven things up. Try a dry erase board or a pad of paper on an easel for visual purposes. Some people learn by listening, but others need to see key points for retention. Vary your speech patterns. I talk fast, so if I slow down my rate of speech a bit, people take notice. Try varying your volume. Raise your voice for emphasis. Lower your voice to make a serious point. Repeat things. Be exciting and interesting to engage your audience. Take a few chances!

Although you're not an actor in a Broadway play or a speaker, per se, it's still a good idea to liven things up a bit. Facts and figures are nice, but sometimes a sales pro needs a little more to grab a customer's attention.

That's just the way it works!

37 PROVE YOUR CLAIMS

A young professional asked me this question recently: *"When I'm speaking to my customer and I'm going through my presentation, what do you reckon she's thinking? What's going through her head?"*

Wow - what a great question from a recent college graduate. There is hope for our institutions of higher learning! Good news since my oldest just left for college…

Unfortunately, you never really know what your customers are thinking.

Of course, you can ask questions (a subject we've covered elsewhere in this book). That's one idea. If you want to know what your customer is thinking – ask. That's always the best approach.

The only other approach is to try to gauge your customer's receptivity through some sort of mind reading. (Sometimes it's all you can do!) If this is all you have, focus this effort on *the conversation going on in your customer's head.*

Think about it - people are naturally suspicious and make many decisions with emotion. It's hard to accurately predict the level of your customer's skepticism, and this is why your ability to prove your claims is important!

Before sharing a hodge-podge of facts and miscellaneous information, consider what you're trying to achieve. The goal is to offer proof and give your customers compelling reasons for changing an attitude or following a specific course of action.

I suggest your proof highlight three critical areas:

Relevance: Does your offering solve the customer's problem or situation? Are you offering something that makes sense – or is needed? This is very important, to say the least, because many sales pros aren't satisfying a "need," except that they "need" their customer to buy something.

Consequences: What's the result of doing what you're suggesting? How will it affect sales, profitability, traffic, etc.? This is a great time to link your customer's decision-making variables to your sales data and facts.

Consistency: Does it all make sense? Does it fit with what's happened in the past? Do you usually deliver what you promise to deliver?

Let's not discount this last element of consistency. You can *prove* your argument until the cows come home, but it won't matter if your word is worthless.

That's just the way it works!

38 REACT WITH GRACE AND DIGNITY

"You're going to regret this!"

That's the response I got from the sales pro when I said "no" to his sales pitch.

I tried to ease the blow. "You made a compelling case, Henry. It's just not the right time for us to take on your brands." (Henry, of course, isn't his real name. I don't want him coming after me...)

But seriously, I was really taken aback. I enjoyed other similarly counter-productive reactions during my days as a retailer, but I remember that one the most.

In the spirit of not making the situation worse when your customer says "no," let's consider some, shall we say, more productive thoughts (or actions) to employ when that happens.

- **React with grace and dignity.** Never react violently, angrily or condescendingly. Similarly, don't let your customer think your life depends on it – even if it does.

- **Determine what kind of "no" you're getting.** Maybe it was the customer's mood that day, so you still have a fighting chance. A soft (hedging) "no" is better than a hard (get out of my face) "No!"

- **Look inward at yourself before blaming somebody or everybody else for the "no."** Consider what you did to help yourself.

- **Learn something about the customer, the market and yourself.** Assess the way you sell and the way your customer buys.

- **Reframe your message/program** to better translate the value proposition of your products.

- **Offer an alternative** – preferably one that you have thought of before the sales call. If your customer isn't buying what you're selling, ask what they are buying.

- **Choose your battles.** Sometimes it's not the right day or the right product. Instead of pushing the envelope when it doesn't feel quite right, save your efforts for more opportune times.

Last, but not least, never let the door close without telling the customer that you're coming back to present yet again. Pretend that "no" actually means "yes, just not right now"!

With that attitude, you'll make the sale next time.

That's just the way it works!

39 REMEMBER NAMES

Have you ever watched a marathon in person? Many marathon runners write their names on their T-shirts so strangers in the crowd will cheer for them and call out their names. The simple sound of hearing names called motivates tired runners as they battle towards the finish line.

If your goal is to build, cultivate and maintain strong customer relationships, knowing people's names is a big part of the equation. This is true not only with your customers, but also with the people at your company with whom you interact on a daily basis. People react with a little "pep in their step" when they hear their names.

Here are some easy ways to help you remember people's names:

- **Make a concerted effort**

I used to have trouble remembering names because I simply didn't try hard enough. Making a concerted effort is half the battle. Concentrate!

- **Observe details**

Look the new person straight in the eye. Really see his or her face. Pick out something unique. Make it a practice to note something about the facial structure, voice, or anything else unique about this person.

- **Repeat the name**

After you hear a new name, call that person by his or her name several times so it will be stored into your long-term memory. Each time you repeat the name, you'll increase the probability of remembering it later.

- **Show your cards**

Admit it if you can't remember someone's name. Don't wing it! Years ago, I was dining in a local restaurant. Someone stopped by my table and mentioned that I had spoken at his company. I replied, "Oh, yeah, I remember you, Tom!" Wrong!! That wasn't his name. I was embarrassed, and he was probably more embarrassed.

- **Use the name**

Use names in passing and on the phone. When passing your associate in the hallway, instead of simply saying, "Hello," say "Hello, Tom!" The result: the person whose name you use will feel good, and his or her name will be reinforced in your mind.

The ability to remember names is essential in both business and social situations. It builds instant rapport and friendship, and it does not cost a penny.

That's just the way it works!

40 SHARE BETTER DATA

Have you noticed how selling has changed over the years?

It used to be relationships were all that mattered. The whole process was kind of shallow. Fact-based selling back then was a sales pro saying to his customer, *"It's a FACT that I need you to buy this!"* Or something like that.

Then in the 1990s, sales experts extolled the virtues of *real* fact-based selling – or *using real data* to support your sales initiatives.

I saw this approach firsthand when I owned a chain of beverage stores. Wholesalers were literally tripping over themselves to show me their data. For the ADD-impaired (me), let me tell you, it was quite annoying.

It was just too much. Frankly, I was overwhelmed by their data.

Reminds me of when you walk up to take a golf shot. You know what happens when you're staring down at the golf ball with all that golf advice running through your head at once? Even if you don't play golf, as I'm sure you can imagine, it's never a pleasant outcome.

That's how I felt with all that data! It was just too much for me to process. Too much information made it impossible to feel like I was making the right decision.

Jump to present day, now we've finally figured out that it's more important to have the right data and the right facts. More is not better— BETTER, MORE SELECTIVE AND TARGETED DATA is better.

Your data can (and should) include sales numbers, market analysis, research, and industry data—really, anything that supports your product's unique selling proposition. It's up to the sales team to gather the most applicable insights and present that data to customers.

It's also very helpful to create compelling stories that relate to your customer's situations…

…But make sure to let the data tell the story. Don't try to fit the data into your story. The last thing you want while sharing data is skepticism and mistrust. I recall many situations where sales professionals tried to shape, mold, structure, and contour data to tell a certain story. It's not play-dough. If you're sharing BETTER data, there will be no need to embellish.

That's just the way it works!

41 SHIFT GEARS WHEN NECESSARY

The following question was posed to me recently.

"Last week, I walked into my customer's office, and he was in no frame of mind to deal with me. I knew from recent observation that he was under extreme pressure and was dealing with a bunch of challenges. When I arrive for a call under these circumstances, how should I handle it?"

What a golden opportunity! YOU can stand out AND use situations like these to your advantage.

Let's examine this question from 30,000 feet.

Unfortunately, most people, most of the time, don't want to do what you want them to do—and certainly not on your timetable. They don't feel your urgency; they're busy with their own priorities and crises.

And when YOU view influence as "getting him to do something," you actually reduce your influence, because you're viewing him as a target, or something to be pushed, pulled, or manipulated. And that never feels good, when you're on the receiving end.

As a sales professional, you're dangerous when you're blinded by your own needs. Even if you want what's best for others, they don't want it (your agenda) shoved down their throats.

So what do you do in this scenario, where your customer clearly has something on his mind and other priorities? How do you get listened to? How can you be the guy who gets paid attention to?

You put your agenda aside for the time being - and step into the other person's world for a spell.

- Say, "You seem to have a lot on your mind today. What's going on?" Or...
- Say, "You seem distracted. What's happening in your world?" Or...
- Say, "Seems like you're going through a difficult time. What's happening?"

And you listen...

If you have some advice or a solution, great! If not, empathy alone will do.

Don't be the sales pro who waltzes in with enormous expectations with little regard for what else your customer has going on. That's not going to get you anywhere.

That's just the way it works!

42 SHOW SOME HUMILITY

"It sucks being the smartest person in the room!"

Those were his words, verbatim. The problem? There were only two people in the room – him and me (the dumb one.) At first, I thought he was joking but NO, it wasn't a joke.

He wasn't even wearing an *"I'm with stupid t-shirt…"*

"Good for you," I thought to myself. "When's the awards ceremony? Are wives invited? It's hard to find a good babysitter on short notice."

This lesson is about an avoidable action that ultimately turns customers against you. Showing too much ego and not enough humility. Thinking (and worse, saying) that you're the smartest person in the room.

It begs a serious question. Is having such incredible intelligence all it's cracked up to be? Is it that important to think so highly of yourself that you would have those thoughts, let alone share such sentiments with others? You can't do everything yourself, can you? Moreover, can having that attitude possibly motivate anybody? That intelligence is a rare breed and you're one of the lucky ones?

I'm afraid it's quite the opposite. When I ran my retail business, I didn't want to be the smartest person in the room. I wanted to be surrounded by talented people. Sure, I had confidence in my abilities, but I understood that with strong contributions from others, we were a much more effective team.

These days, your company needs everyone's contribution so it's best to look for talent everywhere. As a manager or sales professional, it's best to consider what the people around you do best. Consider what they do better than the people around them. Look for tasks they do without being asked – and with little effort. Consider at your customer's staff, as well.

They're surely a talented bunch. You be the one to take a young person under your wing. Let a young star have the credit!

And for the love of humanity, show some humility! You'll get much more from your customers and just about everyone else.

That's just the way it works!

43 SIMPLIFY YOUR PRESENTATIONS

A few years ago, I asked a retailer how his sales professionals could curry more favor with his company.

His answer: **"If my sales professional focuses on helping me achieve my objectives, I'll listen to him all day long!"**

I was struck by the simplicity...

He was saying to simplify your message to include just the basics. Share what will help him and "pitch" (get rid of) the rest.

To clarify, consider a couple of concepts (which might seem controversial):

1) Your customers don't care about your products.
2) Your customers don't care for self-promotional talk.

Have I ruffled a few feathers? I hope so . . . remember, I was a retailer for many years!

The reality is that capturing and keeping your customer's attention requires a Herculean effort. Customers, like it or not, are impatient, easily distracted, forgetful and demanding. They're drained, and they don't want any more complexity added to their lives. Given that, they will always take a greater interest in a professional who is completely focused on addressing their business needs.

So what do you do?

Simplify! Look at your presentation through your customer's eyes.

- If it's **overly complicated**, pitch it. He won't take the time to decipher.
- If it's **not valuable** in some tangible way, pitch it. You'll seem like everyone else.
- If it's not **aligned** with his goals, economic situation or current reality, pitch it. (Unless you come up with a persuasive, well-thought-out plan to help your customer reach a different conclusion.)
- If it's not a **current priority** to your customer, pitch it.

Did I shock you with that last point?

If we only sold to our customer's priorities, most selling activity would grind to a halt and we'd all be really hungry. So, yes, try to make your product a priority; just don't go about it with information overload or unclear messaging in a buzzword-laden presentation. Be different!

Remember my reality when I was a retailer: I desperately needed to protect my time (my scarcest resource). If dealing with a sales professional was overly complicated, or if I couldn't foresee a sizable gap between doing what he recommended and doing nothing, he didn't get the sale.

So, simplify your message and maintain a laser-like focus on what your customer cares about.

That's just the way it works!

44 STAY ON COURSE

I didn't go there for the thrill of victory. I simply wanted to run a local race in our community. So one Sunday morning, I toed the line at the Deerfield Dash 5K. The race started and, lo and behold, I found myself in first place. Could this be the day? Was I going to be forever immortalized in Deerfield Dash lore - someone the locals would always remember?

Uh, no…

The trouble started when I reached an unmarked four-way intersection. I felt like Dorothy in The Wizard of Oz but without the scarecrow there to tell me which way to go! Yep, I went the wrong way, and by the time I figured it out, victory would belong to someone else. I should have looked at the course map prior to the race.

So here's my question for you: Do you have a course map for the busy race known as your day? Consider doing the following and you'll be more likely to stay on course.

1) *Start the day with a brief planning session* - Take some time to contemplate what needs to happen for the day to be considered a success. What's most important? What must get done?

2) *Write out your daily objectives* - Mental notes are vague and ill defined. Putting your objectives on paper pulls your energy to the target.

3) *Write everything down* - Writing down your thoughts, ideas, and to-do's clears the head and allows for more creativity.

4) *Review your notes, plans and objectives as the day goes on* - Your situation is constantly changing. Plus, it's mentally nourishing to see what you've accomplished.

5) *Handle your most important priorities early in your day* – Many people are at their best in the morning, so it's wise to use that time. Plus, if the day goes haywire, at the very least you'll have completed your most important tasks.

6) *Recap the day* - Was what happened what you wanted to happen? What worked well, and what would you do differently next time?

Let's go back to the Deerfield Dash for a moment. I came in with a respectable 3rd place, but I finished behind a man pushing a baby jogger. (Cute kids, though…)

Sadly, had I looked at the map, glory would have been mine. It can be yours, as well, if you stay on course.

That's just the way it works!

45 STAY ON THE RIGHT SIDE OF THE TRACKS

Do you have a competitor who consistently undercuts you by giving away hats, lights, and glasses, not to mention cutting a few pennies off a case here or there? Or have you noticed a situation in which cases seem to "randomly" fall off the delivery truck and miraculously end up in the customer's stock room?

If you're unlucky enough to find yourself in that sort of purgatory, what do you do? Do you cross over to the "dark side"?

Don't!

A good choice is to stay above that nonsense. It's a very slippery slope, and once you start giving away the kitchen sink, the house cannot be far behind.

I suggest the following: Get your team together and pose the following questions: What do we do really well? Why should people buy from us? What are our positives? What might motivate our customers to do business with us because they *want* to, not because they *have* to?

You might come up with some of the following answers:

- Our customers appreciate our flexible delivery policies
- Our customers enjoy the ease in ordering product
- Our customers value that we are constantly sharing relevant product knowledge

- Our customers appreciate that we teach them how to sell premium products
- Our customers see that we maintain their displays, coolers, etc. better than the other guys
- Our customers see that we make more calls than anybody else
- Our customers acknowledge that our sales professionals are the most responsive in the market
- Our customers have unfettered access to our company's leadership

The CEO from a distributor in Illinois suggested that his most educated customers (those who understand the dynamics and attributes of a successful business relationship) are the most likely to be turned off by the kind of back door selling described above. If that is the case in your market, your challenge is to make sure that more of your customers understand what you bring to the table. I'm sure your team can come up a list just like the one above, so whatever you excel in, always make sure to let your customers know.

Sometimes you have to help your customers understand just what you do for them.

That's just the way it works!

46 THINK

Here's something that I've noticed over time: Many people don't really know how to think. When faced with a problem, they'll go to any length to not think. Many ask advice from the most illogical people - like the barista at Starbucks, or members of their family who have no particular experience in their industry. Few of them will take out a notepad, write the problem at the top of the page, put away the smart phone and deliberately open the *thinking* app in their own mind.

Consider what the human mind is capable of. Look at what's happened over the last several years - the inventions, the ingenuity. There's been more advancement in the last 10 years than in the 10,000 years prior to that. Yes, it's very powerful what the mind can do, and as the "Father of Positive Thinking" Earl Nightingale once said about the mind, "The great thing is that we all own one."

Question: Are you using your mind properly?

My suggestion is to take 20-30 minutes a day to exercise your mind. (If you can't do this daily, do it once a week, at the very least.) Take a blank sheet of paper. Write down a problem, goal, customer, etc. List as many ideas as possible for taking a few steps forward. Include ways to build upon what you're already doing, as well as new approaches to make the situation a bit better.

Once you begin putting your ideas to paper, make sure to keep in mind the following:

#1 - This isn't easy, and most of your ideas won't be any good.

#2 - #1 doesn't matter. Write down every idea, no matter how absurd, that pops into your head.

What you're doing in this process is starting your machinery, getting everything oiled up and ready for the day. What you'll find is that your subconscious will continue processing all day, causing ideas to bubble up when you least expect them. When that happens, write them down as soon as you can.

Don't get overwhelmed by seeing an audacious goal at the top of the page. Just think of it as a problem that's waiting to be solved. Thinking about these very challenging goals, you'll be using more of your mental power – which is a positive thing.

But none of this happens without dedicated "thinking time."

That's just the way it works!

47 TURN OFF THE TELEPROMPTER

Do you ever feel that most sales professionals have forgotten how to have a simple conversation? Look around during a sales call, and all you see are spreadsheets, laptops, and iPads, instead of people conversing about business. Many presentations seem staged, canned, and overly rehearsed.

To shake yourself out of this rut, come prepared to ask illustrative questions designed to get your customer to open up a bit.

Asking these kinds of questions may be tough or even feel uncomfortable at first. Many professionals shy away from open-ended or personal questions and instead rely on status quo questions—those designed to gain information that the sales professional should already know before the appointment even starts.

The idea is to ask a question that stops your customer in his or her tracks because it is so intelligent and insightful!

Here are a few examples of illustrative questions:

- Is any aspect of your business surprising you lately?
- You once mentioned that _____ [insert what is important] is most important to you in a beverage partner. Has that changed?
- How did you decide to do _____? (If you notice something unique, new, or different about your customer's premises.)
- What do you think of _____ [choose a competitor's new product]

- What is one part of your selection you would most like to improve right now?
- What are your customers asking for?
- What are your criteria for selecting new products?

And most importantly, as I've mentioned in other places, be careful with PowerPoint.

PowerPoint presentations should be renamed "power plays," because of all the distributors and suppliers who show up with their presentations and literally take over the room, dominating the time with their own propaganda shows.

It serves no one's purpose.

Instead, turn off the teleprompter and ask a few of the above questions. Your presentation will become more than a glorified brag session. And that's a good thing!

That's just the way it works!

48 USE CLOSING STRATEGIES WITH CARE

Have you ever tried the infamous "sending the goods in, even though the customer didn't say YES" closing strategy? I've been on the receiving end of that one many times.

As a retailer, I experienced many different closing techniques. I'm not a big fan of teaching these techniques for the following reasons:

- I find closing techniques to be a bit manipulative.
- I believe that a large majority of successful selling hinges upon whether or not your customer likes and trusts you.
- I believe that if you have conveyed your case confidently and convincingly, and if your customer has a need for the benefits that your product provides, he will pull the trigger. He will show you his intention by his spoken words or unspoken gestures. You just have to be observant enough to see them.
- I believe that closing (a sale) is more a continuation of a long-term relationship than a specific point in time.

That said, I understand the need for sales professionals to take their customers' temperatures to gauge their levels of interest. Although there are many different techniques, we'll concentrate on one. Many experts call it the *trial close*.

The trial close is a way to determine how interested your customer is in what you're selling. The advantage of this technique is that it's not much more than checking your customer's interest earlier in the sales process. The trial close takes away the element of surprise, leaving no confusion as to why you're there and what you're trying to accomplish. You're trying to make a sale. The trial close also helps you keep your mouth closed – so you don't talk your way out of the sale. (I saw that **way** too many times!)

So, make sure to keep things simple and to support your claims with facts and figures. Never sell beyond the limitations of your product. Answer all objections because unanswered objections just create more objections.

However you decide to do it, just make sure to ask for the sale. You are not going to get the sale through mental telepathy.

That's just the way it works!

49 USE POWERPOINT WISELY (PART 1)

I rarely use PowerPoint.

I don't care for the medium much, but I understand that it's a valuable business tool – if you use it correctly.

My issue is that PowerPoint takes the focus away from the presenter and places it, instead, on a dark screen in a dark room. Meetings should be inspirational and motivating. The focus should be on the presenter, the one with the message and conviction to see his company, his people, and his brands succeed—not on a screen most people in the group can't see…

…Or don't want to see!

If PowerPoint is a must, let's consider a few basics.

- **Put some thought into the opening slide.**

Something more original than "Sales Meeting – April 4, 2012." Consider putting a picture of a new sales professional, or a hugely positive sales promotion. Show something to grab the group's attention.

- **Remember, less is more.**

Many decks are between 70-80 slides. Many slides are jam-packed and very hard to read from any distance. So, as you prepare, ask yourself – **is this really something I need to cover or can it be covered in another setting?** Perhaps with an email prior to or after the event.

- **If they can't read it, don't include it.**

Fancy colors, elaborate graphics, and dark shades are all quite difficult to read. As soon as the audience determines that they can't see the information, they'll tune out – quickly.

- **Think more highlights and less detail.**

Instead of placing a detailed table or chart on a slide, share this information in the form of a handout. (Handouts and PowerPoint in the right combination can actually be very powerful and help keep people's attention by mixing it up a bit.) Use your time together to highlight the highlights.

Remember that the focus should be on you – the presenter. If you *play your cards right* (get it? PowerPoint deck?), the three to five takeaways will be obvious to everyone in the room.

That's just the way it works!

50 USE POWERPOINT WISELY (PART 2)

The effective use of PowerPoint is too big a subject for just one lesson! So let's continue the discussion by taking a more detailed look at what your slides actually say and how to present your points and ideas more effectively.

- **Use a transition slide when making a serious point.**

Show numbers and concepts to make your case, but when it comes breaking the data down for the KEY takeaways, put up a transition slide or darken the screen. Yes, I want the group **focused on you**. I want them to see your conviction, your belief. I realize I mentioned this in the last lesson. Take the hint – please! It's important…

- **Tie the slide's title to what's actually on the slide.**

Keep page titles as short as possible and clearly spell out what the slide is sharing. Make the title thought-provoking. It's ok to be provocative. Ask a question. Stimulate conversation, but make sure your points tie to what you're trying to share with THAT slide.

- **Clearly specify the takeaway point.**

If you're trying to make a serious point, allowing your customer to guess the nature of said point is not the way to go. Don't leave it up to one's imagination. Clearly specify the take-away in an easy-to-understand manner.

- **Include an agenda.**

People will go with you much more willingly when they know where they're going. As you consider the flow of your presentation, make sure to include a review of goals and strategies, assessments and updates and, of course, your recommendations.

- **Use rhetorical questions.**

To break up the minutiae, pose a few rhetorical questions. Get the customer thinking. Slides that pose the following questions are great for introducing topics: *What's happening in the market? Why are we seeing these shifts/changes/opportunities? What do we plan to do about it?*

- **Watch for confusion!**

Each day we're inundated with so much information. Our hard drives are pretty overwhelmed, so if YOU review your slides and come away a little confused, imagine how your customer will feel. Give your information in short, manageable chunks. Make sure your information supports your point, and for the love of all in attendance . . . say only what needs to be said. Everyone will be happy, and happy customers are more likely to follow your recommendations.

That's just the way it works!

ABOUT THE AUTHOR

Do you want your sales team to INCREASE sales and BROADEN distribution?

That's a rhetorical question. Of course, you do!

Through his workshops, presentations and training classes, Darryl Rosen will help YOUR sales team *corner sales success.*

Darryl has nearly 30 years of experience in the beverage industry - as a retailer, consultant, and sales and management trainer.

And why should that matter to you? Great question!

Darryl has seen the good and the bad. Moreover, his extensive experience and interactions with thousands of professionals throughout the industry have given him a deep understanding of the dynamics and economics of the business.

100% of Darryl's work is in the beverage industry, so if you want to sell more beverages, he's your man. He's pragmatic in his approach, yet passionate about the message, much like he wants your people to be.

Darryl knows what works and what doesn't work, and he'll make the message come alive for your team.

Visit www.corneringsalessuccess.com for more details.